Whispers of My Heart

Whispers of My Heart
Daughters of the King Bible Study Series
Kathy Collard Miller

Cover Design: Anna O'Brien, Jeff Gifford
Interior Design: Melinda Martin
Editor: Susan K. Stewart
Published in Association with Suzy Q Inc.

PUBLISHED BY: Elk Lake Publishing, Inc., 35 Dogwood Dr., Plymouth, MA 02360

Library Cataloging Data
Names: Miller, Kathy Collard (Miller Kathy Collard) -Title: Whispers of the Heart; Daughters of the King Bible Study Series / Kathy Collard Miller
132 p. 23cm × 15cm (9in × 6 in.)
Description: Elk Lake Publishing, Inc. digital eBook edition | Elk Lake Publishing, Inc. Trade paperback edition | Massachusetts: Elk Lake Publishing, Inc., 2016.
Summary: Don't know what words to say in prayer?
Identifiers: ISBN-13: 978-1-944430-92-4 (POD) | 978-1-944430-93-1 (ebk.)
1. intimate prayer 2. Scripture truth on prayer 3. Words to say 4. Pray like Jesus 5. Draw closer to God 6. Intercession 7. Gratitude and praise

Endorsements

People are talking about Kathy Collard Miller's *Daughters of the King Bible Study Series* and *Choices of the Heart*...

Kathy Collard Miller's *Choices of the Heart* is a Bible study full of sound scriptural principles, balanced spiritual wisdom, and a deep understanding of what matters most to women. Miller's study makes great use of an all-star, all female cast of leaders falling on both sides of the spiritual and moral equation. Her insightful questions invite the reader to reflect on her own life within a scriptural framework—prompting growth from the heart. I can't wait to use *Choices of the Heart* with my own women's bible study.

I'm looking forward to more from Kathy Collard Miller!

Catherine Finger, Ed.D
Superintendent, Grayslake District 127, Grayslake, IL
Speaker and Author of the *Murder with a Message* series

Kathy Collard Miller thoughtfully addresses choices and attitudes that undermine or set us free. With encouragement and warmth, she helps us choose God's way and blessing. This exploration of biblical lives and choices can change your life.

Judith Couchman
Author of *Designing a Woman's Life*
book, Bible study, and seminar

With each lesson, I was invited to recognize that choices of the heart aren't simple or defined without the grace of God. Each account of women in the Bible in this Bible study lifts a layer of possible misconception, asserts refreshing challenges, and presents applications of God's Word, bold yet gentle. At times, the reader is tugged to examine the heart and analyze motives. But with each lesson, the exhortation is profoundly clear, leaving a pleasant reassurance that we women today do have much in common with women of the Bible. Yet, we are called to learn from their examples to make godly choices as daughters of the King who dance to the melody of his redeeming love.

Janet Perez Eckles
author of *Simply Salsa: Dancing Without Fear at God's Fiesta*

As the founder of Modern Day Princess Ministries I am always looking to recommend resources for women that further the depth of our walk with Christ. The Daughters of the King series by Kathy Collard Miller does exactly that. It enables you to discover the wealth you have in knowing the King of Kings as your Heavenly Father and begin walking in the royalty you possess.

Doreen Hanna
Treasured Celebrations, Founder & President
www.moderndayprincess.net

Choices of the Heart provides excellent insight and instruction for the Christian woman who longs for more of God's Word. The women of the Bible come alive as they tackle life issues and struggles that are relevant to today's world. Kathy Collard Miller is a name you can trust for great Bible teaching.

Laura Petherbridge
Speaker and author of *The Smart Stepmom, 101 Tips for The Smart Stepmom*, and *When I Do Becomes I Don't—Practical Steps for Healing During Separation and Divorce*

Kathy Collard Miller's new study, *Choices of the Heart*, gives us a treasure chest of encouragement and wisdom for a glorious life. Whether we struggle with the grittiness of jealousy, temptation or unforgiveness, Kathy points us to God who always gives us the power to move us into a meaningful pathway. I love the way Kathy takes the participant through the journey of examining the lives of women in the Bible and revealing the outcome of their bad and wise choices.

This is a great study for personal reflection during a devotion time or for discussions in a larger group setting. Kathy has done stellar research and written a masterpiece crafted to enrich the reader's knowledge of the Bible and their spiritual life.

Heidi McLaughlin
International speaker and author of *Sand to Pearls, Beauty Unleashed*
and *Restless for More*
www.heartconnection.ca

At the crux of every circumstance, we have two basic choices: whether to trust and whether to obey—intentional decisions to yield to God and embrace his Word. Kathy captures this powerful truth in *Choices of the Heart*. She invites us to walk with God in the great adventure of life, encouraged along the journey by our Heavenly Father's love and faithfulness. Such a motivating study!

Dawn Wilson
Founder of Heart Choices Today
San Diego, California, President of Network of Evangelical Women
in Ministry (NEWIM)

Dedication

I dedicate *Whispers of My Heart* to my precious and
beloved grandchildren, Raphael and Matilda. I pray
you will value the study of God's Word and know
God hears the whispers of your heart.

Acknowledgments

Back in the 1990s, Mary Nelson of Accent Publications saw the potential of my idea for a Bible study series. With her guidance, the twelve-book study in the "Daughters of the King Bible Study Series" was created. I was grateful for her leadership.

Now I'm thrilled Deb Haggerty has understood and supported my vision of expanding the initial simple format to include commentary and greater depth, first through *Choices of the Heart* and now this next one in the series. Thank you, Deb. Your leadership of Elk Lake Publishing is phenomenal and you are the Publisher of the Year in my book! You bless me with confidence and encouragement.

Susan K. Stewart of Practical Inspirations has been a delight to work with as she edited and wisely guided me toward communicating clearly the truths of Scripture. Susan, you have a gentle yet skillful ability, and I so appreciate your responsiveness.

I value having my agent, Shawn Kuhn, on my team of support and wisdom. Thank you, Shawn, for being available.

I'm so grateful for the love and encouragement from my husband, Larry. Honey, let's make it another forty-six years walking this journey together! You make God look good.

Whispers of My Heart

A Ten Lesson Study
in the Daughters of the King
Bible Study Series

Kathy Collard Miller

Elk Lake
PUBLISHING, INC.

Plymouth, Massachusetts

Contents

Lesson 1

JOYFUL FOCUS
On God

Prayer. What joy we experience when we take the time to focus on our great God. Whether we think we pray enough or not, we know we can never spend too much time talking to our heavenly Father.

We know God's Word calls for us to pray, and we sense God's wooing to focus on him, but the challenge comes when any number of obstacles bombard us. We can question whether we're praying in the right way. We can wonder if God hears us. We hear someone else pray beautifully, and we believe we aren't eloquent. We hesitate to pray when others are listening.

The doubts and confusion can swirl around in our minds and hearts and block our confidence in seeking God. And then when our prayers aren't answered the way we asked, we conclude God doesn't love us. We can even claim biblical "promises" about prayer but the answers still seem a part of some big mystery we don't understand.

Truly, there are many blocks and much to learn. The most wonderful thing is God invites us to seek him while he continues to teach us. There is hope.

- How do you define "prayer"?

- Why do you think we should pray?

- What has confused you the most about what other people say prayer is?

- What do these verses say about the purpose of prayer?

  ○ Acts 1:15-24:

In this example, it's instructive that the Apostles first narrowed the possibilities down to two candidates for one to replace Judas. Then they asked God for guidance to choose one of them. These verses show one way prayer includes our own involvement.

Jesus had personally picked each of the disciples in the beginning, so it made sense to them even in the early days of the church, that they should pray to ask him to choose the next man for leadership.

  ○ I Timothy 4:4-5:

Although we can apply this to what we call "saying grace" at a meal, it refers to everything in our lives. In the previous verse (vs. 3), Paul says it refers to marriage. Overall, whatever God has allowed is good and can be received as a good gift as it is dedicated in prayer.

  ○ James 1:5:

Although God wants to give us wisdom about everything, in the context of this particular passage, James says these persecuted Christians should ask for wisdom in how to respond to the intense trials and temptations they are facing.

     ◦   I Peter 4:7:

Of course, we can and should pray whether we're joyful or sad. But in this context, Peter is warning his Christian friends they will be facing a difficult time which requires special seriousness. Peter could be using "the end of all things" to refer to each person as they face death. Or it could refer to some catastrophic event including persecution. Neither Peter nor his readers could have known their "world" of Jerusalem would soon be coming to an end, because its destruction by Nero wasn't far off (70 A.D.).

- Even if we didn't have all those reasons, why should we still pray (Matthew 7:7-11)?

Our loving heavenly Father wants us to know every single concern we have and every part of our lives is of interest to him and can be brought to him in prayer. He only intends to answer and provide whatever is best for us. We may not consider his answer to be for our good at the time, but if we trust him, we can receive his answer with thanksgiving.

- According to I Timothy 2:1-3, Matthew 26:41, and II Thessalonians 3:1-3, what are other purposes of prayer?

In these verses, God communicates even more thoroughly we can bring every person, even those in high standing, to his attention. Whereas very few of us can imagine ever having an audience with an earthly king, we do have access to the King of Kings who is in charge of the activities of everything and all people, including the most influential people on earth.

- Eve's "Daily Quiet Time" was different from ours. She physically walked with God while she talked with him. How did Eve fail to benefit from that privilege (Genesis 3:1-7)?

Eve may have been talking to God but there was someone else talking to her. Sometimes we can mistake Satan's evil whisperings for God's voice.

  ○ How do you think prayer can prevent us from being deceived as Eve was (Genesis 3:13)?

Eve replies to God's inquiry but if she had talked with him as soon as the serpent began to whisper evil ideas, she could have prevented succumbing to the temptation.

  ○ Eve experienced many unpleasant results when she hid from God (Genesis 3:8-16). What results have you seen in your life when you didn't pray about something?

- When we pray, we are the beneficiaries. What are some of those benefits?

  ○ Proverbs 28:13:

  ○ Mark 11:24-26:

  ○ Philippians 4:6-7:

  ○ James 5:13-16:

- ○ I John 1:9:

- ○ Which of those benefits is most meaningful to you?

Although our motive for prayer shouldn't be to gain something, God loves to benefit us. Like a loving father who rewards his children, God, our heavenly Father loves our attention and he loves lavishing blessings on us. When we're blessed, we're also an example of God's love to others.

- What truth does God reveal about prayer in Proverbs 15:29?

- Read John 9:31. Why do you think God does not hear the prayers of unbelievers?

The wicked in effect are saying to God, "I want to be separate from you. I want to do my own thing, so get away." God honors their request. Since those who pray are saying, "Please be with me and help me," God responds to them by drawing close. We are each receiving what we're asking for.

All of us are sinners as Romans 3:23 tells us: *For all have sinned and fall short of the glory of God.* But the "sinner" represented in John 9:31 is the one who rejects God repeatedly and remains in his or her sin, not receiving God's saving grace. Unfortunately, the prayer of the sinner who says, "Get away from me, I want nothing to do with you," will have his prayer answered "yes."

If you want to acknowledge your sin, you can respond in repentance to God and receive his offer of salvation. He is reaching out to you with his gift of forgiveness and cleansing. Pray to him and ask him to forgive you. Tell him you know you deserve spiritual death but you want to claim Jesus' death and resurrection to apply to you. He always hears and responds to that prayer. And then read the Bible, pray often, and find a church which preaches the Gospel—which is the "good news" of Jesus dying on the cross for sinners and how we can depend upon our position in Christ for daily living.

- How do your prayers make God feel (Proverbs 15:8)?

  o Why do you think God values your prayers so much?

  o What "sacrifices" might an unbeliever make to God today?

  o Why do you think the Lord doesn't value the wicked's sacrifices?

The sacrifices of the wicked are unacceptable to God because their motive is not to acknowledge he is their only hope but to appear to do the right thing as they work to earn their own salvation. They then can feel proud thus lacking dependence upon God.

The "upright" are not those who act perfectly, but who have claimed their inheritance in Christ through his sacrificial death on the cross. The upright acknowledge their neediness and approach God with a humble heart.

- After the disciples and followers of Jesus had seen him ascend into heaven, what did they do (Acts 1:12-14)?

  o When we don't know what next step to take, how can their example help us know what to do?

So often when we're unsure of what to do, even in our service to God, we flail about just keeping active doing anything. We might fear if we do nothing our inactivity will be judged negatively by others—and even ourselves. Sometimes it's better to wait on God's further orders and faithfully keep obeying his last instructions.

Not only did the disciples and followers not know what to do, they may have been afraid Jesus' enemies would try to harm them, as they had Jesus. Yet to their credit, if they were afraid, it would have been reasonable—from a human perspective—for them to flee the city and area.

But Jesus had told them to stay put (Acts 1:4) so if they fled, they would have been disobeying him. To their credit, they remained despite the possible danger.

Their response of prayer was a wise one and an example for us. Whether we're confident of God's directions or not, we can pray and continue to seek him.

- The writer summarized the desire of his heart in a prayer expressed in Proverbs 30:7-9. What were his two requests?

   ○ If you had to summarize the desires of your heart in two requests, what would they be? Write them in the form of a prayer.

The writer, who is identified in Proverbs 30:1 as Agur, son of Jakeh, is only mentioned here in the Bible. Commentators believe he lived in the era of Solomon, which of course, is when the biblical book of Proverbs was written. Most of the proverbs in this biblical book were written by Solomon.

The word *agur* is from a Hebrew word meaning "collector" and Agur is indeed known for collecting numerical sayings as this chapter reveals.

- Read Isaiah 26:3-4. How does prayer help us have a steadfast, trusting heart?

- How do the following spiritual principles connect with prayer and what results from each?

Verse(s)	Principle	Connection	Results
Proverbs 3:5-6			
Proverbs 16:2-3			
Matthew 6:16-18			
Matthew 6:33-34			

Verse(s)	Principle	Connection	Results
James 4:6-8			
James 4:13-16			

- What principles of prayer do you see in:

  o Nehemiah 8:2-6:

  o I Kings 8:38-40:

  o Psalm 77:1-3:

  o Psalm 95:6:

Obviously, there are an unlimited number of verses referring to the importance of prayer and the impact God wants to have in our lives through it.

Prayer is most simply two-way communication with God. There are various aspects of it. Whether we are seeking God individually or in a group, whatever the purpose or the need, regardless of the form prayer takes, every time and in every way we pray, God is listening. He loves for his children to seek him and depend upon him.

- The simplest things we do can indicate our attitude toward God. What principle of prayer does Jesus teach in Matthew 14:19, 26:26?

- What can these different kinds of prayer indicate about our attitude toward God?

   o   intercession:

   o   grace for food:

   o   praise:

   o   thanksgiving:

   o   confession:

   o   plea for help:

- How does prayer help to make adjustments in your attitude toward God, toward others, and life's circumstances?

   o   Can you give a specific example?

- Read Matthew 26:36-46. What did Jesus request from his Father (vs. 39)?

   o   Why do you think Jesus didn't want to drink the cup of judgment for sin?

- ○ Regardless of what Jesus wanted, what was his attitude (vs. 39b)?

- ○ What insight does Hebrews 5:7-9 give about the purpose of God's answer of "no" to his Son?

- ○ What should we learn from God's "no" answers to our requests?

Jesus experienced every aspect of being human—except sinning. He completed his Father's will to die for the sins of men. In his humanness, he didn't want to suffer, as any person would respond. Yet, he accepted his father's answer of "no" to his request to be spared. Because he wanted to avoid the pain and the shame, his obedience is highlighted. He could choose to suffer because he trusted his Father's ultimate purpose of the "no": redemption from sin and restoration to God for people would be accomplished. Additionally, he would rise from the dead overcoming the power of death, thus giving hope of heaven to Christians.

The more we can trust our heavenly Father's good plan even when he says no to our requests, the more we can live in peace knowing he'll be glorified.

- • God said "no" to his Son and made our salvation possible. What can we be assured whether God answers us "yes," "no," or "wait"?

  - ○ Jeremiah 29:11-13:

  - ○ Romans 8:35-39:

- ○ Philippians 4:19:

- ○ James 1:17:

- ○ Which of those verses is most meaningful to you?

- ○ How do they encourage you to trust God more?

My precious Princess and Daughter,

I DO LOVE THE TIMES YOU TALK TO ME. Whether you're in trouble and asking for help; whether you're confused and asking for guidance; when you come to me with your praise and thanksgiving; or whether you just want my attention for any reason, I delight in your call to me.

There is joy for both of us when you seek me in prayer. I long for the fellowship of your attention. I wanted it so much, I sent my only Son, Jesus, to die for you to make it possible.

I want you to enjoy our time together as much as I do. I want you to feel loved and approved as we communicate. I look at you with eyes of love and acceptance because you are my precious Daughter.

I know you may not always appreciate or understand my answers to your requests. But please believe, dear one, I only respond with what I know will be best for you. Will you trust my wisdom and permit me to do what is right for you? If you could see the situation the way I do, you'd choose the same thing.

Please continue to seek me. I don't want anything to keep us from our times together. They mean so much to me. And so do you.

Lovingly,

Your heavenly Father, the King

Lesson 2

EFFECTIVE PRAYER
Our Helpers

How wonderful it is to know we can pray at any time and in any place, whether we're jogging, driving, doing housework, even while we're talking to someone else. Our souls can communicate with God with only the whisper of a thought. There are no restrictions to our access to God and there are no barriers that can block us from reaching out to God.

Our heavenly Father provides everything we need and every encouragement to give us the confidence he wants us to know he is ever-present and caring.

One of the primary ways he provides encouragement and confidence is through his Spirit, a part of the Trinity. The Holy Spirit, our resident Helper, is always with us. When we're confused, uncertain, or hurting, the second person of the Trinity, Jesus, pleads our cause before the Father. If you've ever felt unsupported in your desire for prayer, you can't make people support you but God offers everything you need—every One you need.

- Has anyone been instrumental in teaching you to pray or encouraging you to pray?

o   If so, who and how did they do that?

o   Has anyone not been a positive influence in your prayer journey? Explain.

God in his graciousness often puts people in the role of teaching and supporting us in our prayer journey. Unfortunately, some people can be a negative influence. Even though God allowed that unfortunate example, he always has a plan and a purpose. Even a poor example can motivate us to seek God.

• Why does the Holy Spirit pray for us (Romans 8:26)?

o   When we don't know God's will or how to pray, what can we count on (vvs. 26-27)?

o   How does knowing about the Spirit's support make you feel?

o   Does it influence your attitude about prayer in any way?

God doesn't pour contempt on our weaknesses. In a strange way, our weakness can bring a positive response of seeing our need of an almighty God who cares about every area of our lives—significant or insignificant.

Do you notice in Romans 8:26 there's no definition of "weakness"? Some of us were taught in childhood we only need to bring "big" needs to God because we should handle the *little* weaknesses or trials ourselves. Some heard "God helps those who help themselves."

There are no such distinctions in Scripture regarding prayer or God's desire to respond. Whether our "weakness" is big or little, or we are capable of handling life or not, God wants us to seek him for every need and circumstance. He wants our strength to come from him (Philippians 4:11).

The same encouragement applies to when we don't know what to ask for. After we ask, God never says, "Wrong! Too bad! You didn't ask for the right thing. Away from my sight!"

Unfortunately, our hearts can be so wounded from childhood we fear God's response. Maybe someone shamed us if we said the wrong thing. Or never granted our requests because we didn't ask correctly or with a perfect attitude. God affirms the truth he isn't like that. He understands our weaknesses because he created us. Our weaknesses are intended to draw us in neediness to him.

- What else does the Spirit do for us (Ephesians 1:13-14)?

A seal is used on documents to confirm their validity. It's also used on a piece of communication like a scroll to assure it wasn't opened by the servant who delivered it. Only the person who is the intended recipient can open it.

Likewise, spiritually, the Holy Spirit identifies the validity of the "contract" of salvation God has done in our hearts. And it confirms God as the only one who will be able to receive us, without it being touched by another, like Satan.

- Indicate in the chart from Hebrews 7:25-8:5 how Jesus, as our High Priest, is contrasted with the Old Testament priest (not every verse will cover both). (For a deeper study, you may want to study the Old Testament role and significance of the priesthood and High Priest. See Exodus 20:12-15; Leviticus 1:1-5; Numbers 1:47-53, 16:9-10, 18:1-6)

	Jesus, the High Priest	Old Testament Priests
vss. 23-24		
vs. 25		
vs. 26		
vs. 27		
vs 28		

○ Add other verses and contrasts as you see them.

○ Which characteristic of Jesus as your High Priest do you appreciate the most? Why?

- Why does Jesus have the authority to pray for us (Ephesians 1:20-22)?

  o vs. 20:

  o vs. 21:

  o vs. 22:

- What happens to our prayers?

  o Revelation 5:8c:

  o Revelation 8:3-4:

- Why do we need to depend upon the Holy Spirit and Jesus in prayer (Revelation 12:10)?

  o Does it surprise you that you have a spiritual enemy? Why or why not?

  o How have you seen evidence of Satan's attacks?

  o Did you ask for the Spirit's help? Why or why not?

We do indeed have a spiritual enemy who works in a variety of ways to try to kill and destroy us (John 10:10) because he hates God Almighty. His main evil strategy is through lies and Jesus called him the "Father of Lies" (John 8:44). Therefore, it's imperative we pay attention to the flaming darts of lies (Ephesians 6:16) he sends us. Only by taking *every thought captive to obey Christ* (2 Corinthians 10:5c) can we fight against him effectively.

- Read Job 1:1-2:10. What is Satan's purpose?

    ○ on earth:

    ○ in heaven:

    ○ What do verses 1:12 and 2:6 indicate about God's power over Satan?

    ○ Was Satan right about Job?

    ○ How did Job's wife fail the test?

From an outward appearance, Job was a failure. His good friends even came to tell him so. But God knew the truth and knew Job's heart. We can take great comfort in knowing regardless of Satan's attacks which could include other people misunderstanding us and our motives, God knows our hearts and doesn't expect us to be perfect (Philippians 1:6).

- How do these verses motivate you to call upon your Helpers (the Holy Spirit, Jesus your High Priest, and God the Father) when Satan attacks and accuses you?

    ○ Romans 8:1:

    ○ I Corinthians 10:13:

    ○ Hebrews 12:1-4:

    ○ James 4:7:

- I Peter 4:12-13, 5:10:

- I Peter 5:8-9:

- Which verse is most meaningful to you and why?

- How is Deborah an example of a woman who called upon the Spirit to help her (Judges 4:4-7)?

- Daniel is another person who depended upon God in prayer. Even a royal decree with a death sentence for disobedience could not keep him from his time with God. Read Daniel 6:10-11; 10:11-13.

  - Why was Daniel praying?

  - What immediately happened when he prayed?

  - What prevented God's answer from reaching Daniel?

  - What broke the impasse?

  - What does this passage demonstrate about the importance of calling upon our Helpers as we pray in spiritual battle?

It might seem like we as common believers are not important enough, in comparison to someone like Daniel, to have our prayers blocked. But any believer is powerful in God's kingdom because

God doesn't value one person's prayer more than another's. We can't make a lot of conclusions from the one verse of Daniel 10:13 because there aren't other Scripture giving us more information on this topic. But we can be assured our prayers are always heard and God is strong enough to provide the answer regardless of any obstacles.

- How do you define spiritual battle?

    ○ How do Ephesians 6:18 and Jude 20 give us tools for that spiritual battle?

    ○ What do you think those tools mean?

- The more we pray, the more the Holy Spirit affects our lives. When we pray, what effects will we see (Galatians 5:22-23)?

- Look at Jude 8-23. Compare the lives of those who don't seek our Helpers with those who do.

Those without Spirit (vss. 18-19)	Those praying in the Spirit (vss. 20-23)

Those without Spirit (vss. 18-19)	Those praying in the Spirit (vss. 20-23)

- Use Jude 24-25 as an example to praise and thank God for his promises. Write out your prayer.

- In what ways do you want to concentrate this week on allowing the Holy Spirit to be your Helper in prayer?

If you are ever tempted to believe you aren't supported in your Christian walk, you can be assured you are not alone. The Trinity— Father, Son and Holy Spirit—hears you, cares about you, and promises to work in and through you. Satan may try to convince you otherwise, but your faithful God gives you many evidences of his responsiveness.

My precious Princess and Daughter,

WHEN YOU PRAY, YOU DO NOT PRAY ALONE. My Spirit cries within you. And my Son sits at my right hand interceding for you. We want our best for you. We know you don't always know that. Sometimes you don't even know what to pray for.

The accuser, Satan, comes before me but I know the truth about you. He thinks he's tattling on you—as if I don't know everything. He thinks he will sway me away from loving and accepting you unconditionally. But that's impossible. Absolutely impossible. Please hear me when I promise you have immediate, continual access to my throne. You are my child and my Princess.

Your performance has nothing to do with me hearing you because Jesus died on the cross for your sins to wipe away any separation between us. My Son and my Spirit are your ever-present Helpers.

Talk to me. Our times of close fellowship are important to me—and to you. I see Jesus' robe of righteousness wrapped around you, and you are acceptable and perfect in my sight. Have no fear. I have not left you helpless. Remember, we are in you and we are much greater than Satan.

Lovingly,

Your heavenly Father, the King

Lesson 3

POWERFUL PRAYER
Its Characteristics

What a thrill it is when we see answers to our prayers. Prayer is powerful. At times, though, reaching out to God seems like efforts in futility. They seem to bounce back at us right off the ceiling. Maybe there isn't an answer at all—it seems. Or what occurs isn't what we expected, wanted, or believe is best. We can doubt our relationship with God or distrust he wants the best for us and those we love.

Our Enemy tries to whisper lies like he did to Eve: *Did God really say that?* In these occasions, he adds *You can't possibly believe God cares about you. How ridiculous! See? The answer isn't what you wanted at all.*

That's when we need to remind ourselves how to pray powerfully.

- When was the last time you had a specific prayer answered?

    ○ What was the answer and how did you know it was God's answer?

- When our prayers aren't answered, or it seems like God's answer is always "no" or "wait," we can begin to feel like Naomi. Read Ruth 1. What evidence did Naomi give for her belief God hadn't answered her prayers?

    - Scan chapters 2-4. Although prayer is not specifically mentioned, how does God intervene in Naomi's life?

    - Has there been a time when it didn't seem like God was answering your prayers, yet later you discovered he was? Explain.

The book of Ruth starts out with the depths of Naomi's despair and ends with her surpassing joy. Naomi doesn't seek God directly and yet he graciously and mercifully provides for her and Ruth. So many times, God is more at work than we realize and we're living a Naomi story. God delights to take good care of us, but we don't always give him the credit he deserves. Let's commit to truly trusting him as a good God.

- Several women asked God and Jesus for answers. Match their story with a characteristic of powerful prayer explained by Jesus in these verses: Mark 11:22-24, Mark 5:34, John 14:14-15, Luke 11:5-10.

	Woman	Characteristic & Verse(s)
Genesis 16:7-14		
I Samuel 1:1-20		
Matthew 15:21-28		
Mark 5:25-34		

- Of that information, which is most meaningful or inspiring to you?

- What other characteristics make prayer powerful and important?

  - Matthew 5:23-24:

  - Matthew 6:14-15:

- ○ Romans 12:12:

- ○ I Thessalonians 5:17:

- ○ I John 5:14-15:

- ○ Which of these need strengthening in your prayer life?

God is never discouraged if an aspect of our prayer life isn't as strong as it could be. We are usually critical of ourselves and God isn't cheering for our self-contempt, like we might think. He knows how he will continue to strengthen our walk with him and our prayer life. If you're tempted to compare yourself to anyone you know, or some well-known Christian person, or even people in the Bible, resist. God doesn't compare you nor does he criticize you. But he is looking for opportunities to teach you and urge you on.

- • What is God's purpose in answering our prayers according to John 15:16?

- ○ What does Galatians 5:22-23 indicate is that fruit?

- ○ What do you think is the purpose then of the fruit?

In the time of Jesus, a "teacher" or "rabbi" did not appoint or chose his disciples/followers. A man would choose the person he wanted to learn from. In John 15:16, Jesus changed that practice. He picked the ones he wanted and according to Ephesians 1:4, Christians are chosen by God with the purpose of bringing him glory. He is glorified by having his followers make his nature and power known through the good fruit of righteousness in their lives. The purpose of answered prayer is not for our benefit—although that happens. The ultimate purpose is to fulfill the plans God has determined which will glorify him.

- What is one possible temptation about prayer (Matthew 6:5-7)?

    ○ What is the solution?

    ○ What inward character change do you think can then occur?

    ○ What do you think are "empty phrases" (vs. 7)?

    ○ What do people think "empty phrases" will gain them—(Matthew 5:5, 7)?

    ○ But what important truth does Matthew 5:8 give to counteract long or inappropriate praying?

    ○ How do you determine when to pray in secret and when to share a prayer request?

Fear can block us from praying out loud in a group. We fear being judged because we said something with the wrong words, or in the wrong way, or with too many words. These fears are usually because we don't want others to think poorly of us.

Fear takes the focus off connecting with God and focuses on ourselves. We can even know our motive and feel bad about it. But maybe we were shamed in some way in the past about praying or the way we speak and now we want to avoid pain.

Ask God to develop your strength to trust he only needs to approve or be pleased by your words. Sometimes he just asks your obedience in speaking out in faith and rejecting any condemning thoughts, remembering God focuses on your heart which no one else can see. Let his understanding and compassion comfort and strengthen you.

When prayer requests are shared in a group and the opportunity to pray is available, some feel compelled to pray for every request but praying for everything can limit the opportunity for others to participate. If we fear some request won't get covered, we can trust God to respond to the needs of every person, regardless of whether it's specifically prayed for.

In one regard prayer isn't "needed" since God knows everything and knows what is best for each person. But God allows us the privilege and joy of being involved through praying for others. Sometimes remembering God already knows everything will diminish the need to say too much.

- What elements of prayer did Jesus give in Matthew 6:9-13?

    o   vs. 9:

    o   vs. 10:

    o   vs. 11:

    o   vs. 12:

    o   vs. 13:

- What adds to the power of our prayers (Matthew 18:19-20)?

  - What do you think that means in relation to Matthew 6:5-6?

- What is the significance of the phrase "in my name" (vs. 20)?

Some people believe and teach we can pray for anything we want and God must do it. But imagine for a moment being in a group where someone mentions a need and someone else sitting there has the capability of granting the request. The benefactor knows the request is not the best thing and says so. But the one with the need demands the benefactor grant it.

God only wants us to ask for what he wants to grant. Of course, we don't always know what is best and we can ask anyway. But having the heart attitude of trusting God to give the loving thing, we won't struggle with disappointment or distrust if God refuses our request.

- What attitudes should accompany our prayers?

  - Psalm 95:1-6:

  - Jeremiah 29:11-14:

  - Colossians 4:2:

  - Philippians 4:6-7:

- ○ Hebrews 4:16:

- ○ Which of these do you feel strongest and weakest in?

• When we come before God, what two things should we believe to please God (Hebrews 11:6)?

• What attitudes did Jesus' mother, Mary, have when she responded to God's call in her life (Luke 1:46-55)?

- ○ Considering the consequences of being misunderstood as a pregnant, unmarried woman in her society, how is her prayer remarkable?

- ○ How does she inspire you in prayer?

At times when we are called upon to pray in a way seemingly dangerous, it's very difficult to surrender. One of the hardest prayers is praying for a loved one who is not following God. To say, *whatever it takes, Lord,* is asking God to take steps we might think are dangerous or won't work. But the heart of surrender says, *God, you know best and I trust you,* as Mary prayed.

• What spiritual tool can make our Christian walk more successful and our communion with God more powerful (Psalm 119:9-11)?

- ○ What have you found helpful for incorporating that tool into your life?

- ○ How do you think this tool deepens a Christian's prayer life?

- From today's lesson, how can you make your prayers more powerful?

Our heavenly Father's heart is to hear from us, yet he knows we are hindered by many things. His joy is to provide encouragement for us through his Word. We can cast aside our fears as we trust in him, and we can take hold of the instruction he gives us to have a more vibrant prayer life.

My precious Princess and Daughter,

I WANT YOU TO COME BEFORE ME WITH YOUR REQUESTS AND BE CONFIDENT YOU WILL SEE MY ANSWERS. I made prayer possible because I want my power to be demonstrated in your life. You feel my love and presence when you pray. And you see my power when you see answers. But even if you don't, I'm still attentive to you.

I want you to trust me enough to know my "requirements" for prayer increase your dependence and faith. Yes, I do want you to be clean from sin to have access to my presence. But I want you believing I hear and respond the right way. So, talk to me boldly and confidently. I want my throne room to feel very comfortable and inviting to you. And the more often you enter it, the more comfortable it will be to you. Tell me everything on your heart and mind. Then listen for my whisper in your heart, through others' counsel, and primarily through my Word, my love letter to you.

I want to answer you, dear one. If I'm silent at times, know the answer is coming. Although I can't guarantee you'll understand or see clearly all my answers on this earth, please believe I love and value you. I hear every word, see every tear, know every longing of your heart. I will answer.

Lovingly,

Your heavenly Father, the King

Lesson 4

INTIMATE CONVERSATION
Two-Way Communication

Prayer isn't just talking to God, it's listening too—listening for his response and seeking his empowering. We may not always hear him or understand the answer, but when we do, we are drawn even closer in devotion and commitment—if we are willing to obey.

Sensing God's leading can be a very difficult challenge. In this lesson, we'll see how God responded to the obstacles his servants experienced. Sometimes, those challenges are our very own belief system and the lies we receive as truth. God wants to reach out to us regardless. Let's be open.

- What are the greatest helps and the greatest hindrances you find in hearing God's voice?

    ○ Helps:

    ○ Hindrances:

Read Exodus 3:1-4:18

- Sometimes God speaks to us in dramatic ways. How did God get Moses' attention (3:2-4)?

    ○ What attitude did God want Moses to have about his presence (3:5-6)?

    ○ Do you think we can ever become too "friendly" with God or too presumptuous? Explain.

    ○ How did God want Moses to serve him (3:7-10)?

Although it might not be in the same way—through a burning bush—God may use something strange and unusual to get our attention. God knew Moses needed a dramatic demonstration. He knows what each of us needs to communicate with him. No, it may not be as clear or dramatic as the burning bush, but if we'll be attentive, he might be more obvious than we think or expect. It's up to us whether we will respond. It took a lot for Moses to let God work through his objections. Maybe that's why the dramatic God-entrance was needed. Moses had a lot of layers wrapped around his heart as we'll see.

- What were Moses' reactions during his conversation with God and what were God's answers?

	Moses' Reaction	God's Answer
3:11-12		
3:13-22		
4:1-6		
4:10-12		
4:13-17		

- What did Moses finally do (4:18)?

- Do you identify with Moses in any of those ways when you converse with God? Explain.

- Which of God's responses seems to speak to your heart the loudest?

As stubborn and sinful humans, our selfish needs and our doubts get in the way of truly believing God is answering our prayers for our best. Moses must have sensed danger in God's invitation and commands. After all, he didn't know whether he was still being considered a murderer back in Egypt. He most likely still regarded himself as a coward for running away. Besides, who was he? Merely a shepherd.

In any number of ways, we can regard ourselves incapable of fulfilling something God is asking—whether it's helping in the nursery at church, sharing our faith, or speaking before a group.

We could even feel God has put us on the shelf. Moses went from being a Prince of Egypt to tending sheep. Originally as a prince, he thought he would deliver the Israelites and they would be glad. God stripped the opportunity from him due to a lack of self-control.

God used forty years of shepherding to prepare him for years of shepherding a rebellious "flock" of Israelites. No wonder he was called "meek." Even if God leads us to times of inactivity, it doesn't mean we haven't heard him or he's forgotten us. We can be assured he'll guide us if we'll continue to be open to hearing him.

- Sometimes God speaks to us in less dramatic ways. Read I Kings 19:1-18. How would you characterize Elijah's mental and spiritual states at this time?

  ○ Why do you think God spoke to Elijah with the sound of a soft voice instead of other, more dramatic ways?

- ○ What tone of voice do you think God used in questioning Elijah (vss. 9, 13)?

Our great God is a creative and gentle God. He reaches out to each of us according to what will most woo us and clearly communicate with us. We may not recognize his work all the time and we might think *if only he communicates in this way*, we'll hear him. But he knows our hearts. Moses needed a burning bush because he was convinced God couldn't use him. Elijah's spirit was too wounded to face a fearsome burning bush, so God whispered.

Resist judging how God should respond to someone and don't compare his manner of communication with you based on someone else's experience. He knows what's best for each individual.

- In what ways have you been tempted to compare your prayer life to others?

  - ○ What does Psalm 46:10 indicate is a way to know God and to hear his voice?

- Of the following hindrances, which stop us being quiet enough to hear God's voice, write down a number between 1 and 5 for each thing, indicating its distracting influence in your life (1 being least):

  - ○ children's needs:

  - ○ husband's needs:

  - ○ friends' needs:

o   schedule restraints:

o   busyness:

o   lack of interest:

o   believing prayer is boring:

o   believing prayer is ineffective:

o   having trouble understanding or seeing God's answers:

o   feeling fearful about coming before God:

o   feeling prayers are not important enough to be heard:

o   sin blocking conversation:

God doesn't condemn us for these obstacles. He doesn't give up on us if we struggle or have wrong priorities. He continues to call us to listen and hear, even if the time spent seems insignificant to us.

•   Sometimes we wonder whether we're hearing God's voice or Satan's. Write God's response or action in the last column.

Satan	Truth	God
Accuses and condemns	Romans 8:1, 33-34	
Threatens to withdraw love	Psalm 89:32-34	
Requires perfection	Psalm 103:14	
Brings thoughts of defeat	Philippians 1:6	
Makes world sound inviting and longlasting	I John 2:15-17	
Says there is a limit to God's forgiveness	I John 1:9	

Satan	Truth	God
Tempts and hopes for defeat	James 1:13-14	

Which of those truths gives you hope or direction today?

How would you apply one of the truths to recognizing God's communication with you?

- In order to fight Satan's destructive messages, what do we need to do (II Corinthians 10:3-5)?

  o In practical terms, what do you think this means?

  o How does Philippians 4:8 give further direction for doing that?

An easy and effective way of applying II Corinthians 10:5 is to evaluate each thought as if it were an arrow coming toward our minds and hearts. If we believe every thought coming to us is already "ours," we can falsely believe wrong ideas are already "us."

But if we recognize each "arrow" of thought as something we have a choice to agree with, we can *take it captive* by grabbing it mentally. Then ask ourselves, *Is this the truth? Does this agree with the Word of God?* If it is not the truth because it doesn't agree with God's Word, we can cast it away and refuse to agree with it. If it's a sinful thought, we haven't sinned because we haven't received it.

Even Jesus had what could seem as "sinful thoughts" of temptation from Satan (Matthew 4:1-11). But he refused to agree with them. He counteracted them with truth. We can do the same.

• Write down several temptations or lies Satan consistently throws at you. For each one write a Scripture verse(s) that counteracts it with the truth. See the example.

Lie or Temptation	Scripture	Truth
"You are worthless."	Psalm 139:13-16	God sees me valuable as his creation.

- Even though Satan's messages seem strong at times, of what can we be assured?

  - Romans 8:38-39:

  - I Corinthians 15:57-58:

- What is God's primary way of speaking to us?

  - II Timothy 3:16-17:

  - Psalm 19:7-11:

- What's another way for you to hear his guidance?

  - Proverbs 11:14:

  - Proverbs 12:15:

- Read I Samuel 1. What is Hannah's spiritual and emotional state?

  - How did Hannah get an answer to her prayer?

  - Why did Hannah believe her prayer would be answered "yes"?

God may want to guide us and communicate with us through other people giving us direction or advice. Or another person may confirm an idea we were considering as possibly from God. Hannah believed God led Eli to tell her God's will. God in his gentleness knew she was so distraught it was difficult for her to hear him so he provided counsel through a trusted priest. God will do whatever it takes to communicate with us. It's up to us to be willing to receive what he says.

- God also answers our prayers through the circumstances he allows in our lives. Read Genesis 24. Why do you think Rebekah felt comfortable going to a man, Isaac, she did not know, with a stranger, Abraham's servant?

- Why do you think Laban and Bethuel made the comment they did (vs 50)?

It might not be clear because the names might be unfamiliar to us, but Laban and Bethuel are male relatives. Bethuel can be either Laban's father or brother, commentators aren't sure. Regardless, it was the men of a family who made decisions like who Rebekah would marry. Laban who, in time, proves himself to be greedy and deceitful must have loved seeing the jewelry Abraham's servant gave Rebekah. The jewels most likely were "evidence" enough of God's will—for Laban may have thought there would be some benefit to him in the future being aligned with wealthy Abraham. Both men also saw God's hand leading because of the unusual circumstances of Rebekah meeting the servant at the well.

- Making decisions based only on circumstances is risky, but when the circumstances agree with God's Word and the counsel of other godly men and women, what validity can they have?

- How do the following verses support the importance of circumstances in discerning God's direction?

    ○ Isaiah 14:24:

    ○ Isaiah 25:1:

    ○ Daniel 2:20-22:

- If you are currently seeking God's voice or answer to prayer, what do the following verses promise?

    ○ Deuteronomy 4:29-35:

    ○ Psalm 37:4-5:

    ○ Isaiah 41:10:

- What promises do we have in these verses?

    ○ Isaiah 55:8-9:

    ○ James 4:2-3:

    ○ I John 1:8:

    ○ Why do God's answers sometimes seem undesirable even though we have those promises?

- From the insights in this lesson, what will you incorporate to hear God's answers and leading more clearly?

Let it be clear, hearing God's voice and knowing his will and his ways aren't usually easy. It's a challenge and God doesn't expect us to be perfect in sensing his leading. But he loves hearing us ask him, seek him, and depend upon him, no matter how imperfectly we follow him.

My precious Princess and Daughter,

MY DAUGHTER, YOU ARE IMPORTANT TO ME. I know how much your hectic life and busy schedule can distract you from hearing my voice, but I want to communicate with you and respond to you. Hearing my words does take time and patience; it also involves learning to recognize my whisper in your heart. But don't worry, I am patient with you. I keep trying and I have every confidence you will grow in hearing me better and better, too.

There are many "voices" competing for your attention. I know you won't always recognize my voice among them, even with many years of practice and awareness. But trust me. It is part of my plan because life is a journey in faith. So, don't be discouraged if it seems you'll always question whether it's my voice or not. I'm with you to guide you through life's maze.

Believe me, I am in complete control. Never fear. Keep seeking me. Study my Word, know my heavenly principles, and trust me. My gentle and kind voice will draw you.

Lovingly,

Your heavenly Father, the King

Lesson 5

OBSTACLES
Tearing Down Barriers

Every single one of us faces obstacles in our spiritual life and particularly in our prayer life. Although we can hear of others or observe their prayers and conclude they don't struggle, the truth is most of us believe we could be more effective pray-ers.

The struggle can be a good thing. In a crazy way, dissatisfaction can be useful for then we'll hunger for more connection and communication with God. He can put a desire into us as a means to make us more desperate for him. The problem is if we believe the lies of Satan saying we are hopeless or helpless to make changes.

With our great God, there is always hope. His Word assures us in many ways he hasn't given up on us. He wants to empower us to overcome whatever blocks us from enjoying and benefiting from focus on him.

- What obstacles do you find to having a powerful and consistent prayer life?

- Read Genesis 27:1-28:5. What was Rebekah's fear (27:10)?

° What could Rebekah have done instead of trying to manipulate the situation?

° Do you find the temptation to control people and circumstances easier to fall into when you haven't prayed?

° How does prayer give strength and courage to trust in God?

The Bible doesn't tell us much about Rebekah's prayer life or the kind of relationship she had with Jehovah. In our last lesson, we saw how Rebekah was a young woman who left her home to follow a stranger to marry a stranger. How's that for courage?

Could it be her courage became a sinful strategy to control life? She married Isaac, a mild-mannered man. Had she learned to become manipulative because he didn't get things done? Or he seemed to make unwise choices?

Such difficult circumstances and relationships occur in homes and marriages even today. A wife who has strong opinions may feel she has to take hold and make sure God's will is fulfilled.

May Rebekah's story be a warning if we are tempted to overstep God's instructions for us as wives. God can overcome any unwise choice our husband makes. Of course, God wants us to be a helpmeet with a voice. We do have opinions and wisdom to share. But after voicing them, we can trust God will sovereignly complete his will. How he would have fulfilled his plan for Rebekah's sons we don't know. But she could have trusted he would without becoming the master manipulator with disastrous results.

- Read John 4:1-30, 39-42. What was the Samaritan woman's initial hindrance in talking to Jesus?

    o   vs. 9:

    o   vss. 11-12:

    o   vs. 17:

    o   vss. 19-20:

    o   vss. 25, 27:

    o   Do you find any of the same hindrances when you talk with God?

    o   What finally helped her overcome her obstacles (vss. 23, 26, 29)?

    o   What helps you concentrate in prayer in spite of obstacles?

The Samaritan woman's communication with Jesus is a precious example of how God responds to you and me. We can sense Jesus' love and care for her. The effort he took to make sure he met her is incredible. He didn't "have to" go through Samaria. Almost all Jews didn't. The Jews despised Samaritans because of a long history of problems between them. Jews traveled out of their way to make sure they didn't have any contact with Samaritans. Yet Jesus choose the path others avoided to assure this lonely and hated woman was touched by her Savior.

The reason she was at the well by herself is because all the other women went to the well in the morning when it was cool. They gathered to gossip and share stories—as women do. Unfortunately, they often gossiped about *that* woman—the one with multiple husbands who was considered immoral and an outcast.

Jesus didn't initially reach out to them. They would have been smug in their righteousness. But he knew this needy one would respond to his offer because of her physical and spiritual thirst.

If you feel like an outcast in some way, or unworthy to talk with God in prayer, take encouragement from the Samaritan woman. Jesus wants to hear from you and seeks you as much as he did that woman at the well.

- What do the following verses from Proverbs indicate are hindrances to effective prayer?

  - 15:29:

  - 16:2:

  - 28:9:

  - 28:13:

- What truth about prayer does Luke 18:1-8 teach?

  - How is the widow in Jesus' parable an example for you?

○ Is there anything you've given up praying for, even though you believe it is God's will? If so, why?

○ What new commitment do you want to make regarding that?

It's certainly true we can't claim a prayer must be answered the way we want just because we want it. At times, we'll even think something is God's will and it's not. But we can pray with an attitude saying, *Lord, I'm praying for this because I think it's your will. But I could be wrong. I trust the answer doesn't depend upon my insistence, but upon what will bring glory to you. I trust you.*

Complete the chart, indicating the wrong and right attitudes and motives for prayer.

Wrong Attitudes/Motives	Right Attitudes/Motives
Matthew 6:1-2	Matthew 6:3-4
Matthew 6:5	Matthew 6:6
Matthew 6:7	Matthew 6:8

Wrong Attitudes/Motives	Right Attitudes/Motives
Luke 20:46-47	James 4:8
James 4:2	James 4:10
James 4:3	I John 3:22

- ○ Which wrong attitude or motive affects your prayer life most?

- ○ Which right attitude or motive will you concentrate on this week?

No one has the right attitude or the right motive all the time regarding prayer. Every single one of us struggles in some way at some time. Although discouraging, God doesn't require perfection. Expecting perfection from ourselves can become an obstacle in itself. If we could become perfect in prayer, we'd most likely only be judgmental of others who haven't "gotten it together." Our neediness, like the Samaritan woman at the well, makes us thirsty for God.

Obstacles | Tearing Down Barriers

- Read Mark 9:14-29. Compare verse 24 with James 1:5. In what way do these verses seem to conflict?

  ○ Does James 1:7-8 give any insight for this dilemma?

  ○ Why do you think Jesus healed the son if his father didn't have complete faith?

  ○ What quality of God is demonstrated in the boy's healing?

This needy father with a needy son had most likely sought help from many sources—to no avail. Even when he seeks Jesus' help, the initial response is the worst possible—the demon becomes even more active. How like spiritual growth. It feels like two steps backward and only one step forward.

Jesus questions the father yet Jesus knows the answers already. How like a loving Savior to involve himself in the life of the needy. Can you recognize God cares for your soul by involving himself in your life?

Talk about not doing prayer "right." The father says *if you can do anything*. In that moment, any number of us watching from the crowd would think, *Wrong thing to say. How insulting. Jesus won't help now.*

But no, Jesus doesn't rebuke him, but points him to greater faith in order to have the father express what little faith he does have. The father is humble and honest. Those are characteristics of a heart seeking God.

We can be encouraged. Even though our faith is weak and imperfect, Jesus cares and hears our prayers and responds to our needs. In this case, he gave the father what he wanted and it brought God great glory. We may not always receive the answer we want, but we can still grow in our faith and trust knowing we don't have to be perfect in the way we pray. The word "all" in James 1:8 clarifies it's the person who rejects faith in God *in all his ways* who won't see God's answers. God may not answer or a double-minded person may not recognize God's work.

- Why does Mark 14:38 link prayer and temptation?

  o What is the obstacle to powerful prayer and resisting temptation indicated?

  o Have you ever experienced a time when prayer made you strong enough to resist temptation? Explain.

- How does prayer relate to marriage?

  o I Corinthians 7:5:

  o I Peter 3:7:

  o What part does prayer play in your marriage?

- Read Matthew 5:3-10. How do you think each of the following attitudes help to encourage prayer?

  o vs. 3, being poor in spirit:

  o vs. 4, mourning:

- ○ vs. 5, being meek:

- ○ vs. 6, hungering and thirsting for righteousness:

- ○ vs. 7, being merciful:

- ○ vs. 8, being pure in heart:

- ○ vs. 9, being a peacemaker:

- ○ vs. 10, being persecuted:

- ○ Which attitude do you need to grow in? How will you practice that?

Your loving heavenly Father and his Son Jesus want you to be encouraged to seek him regardless of the obstacles you face. He loves to hear from you and wants to help you overcome anything diminishing your desire or ability to pray. And remember, only the imperfect need to think about praying. (That's all of us!)

My precious Princess and Daughter,

LIFE CERTAINLY SERVES UP SOME HEFTY HINDRANCES TO TALKING TO ME, DOESN'T IT? That's because Satan, my enemy and yours, is the prince of sin and of the earth—for now. He uses many obstacles to try to prevent our fellowship. But I know them all, and I'm much stronger than any of them. So be assured, they will not separate us—unless you let them. You will know my will as you spend time talking with me and studying my words in the Bible. However, it may not always be perfectly clear or the answer you want.

Make sure unconfessed sin and disobedience aren't causing a break in our fellowship while on this earth. You can do something about those hindrances. I expect you to. And know nothing will separate us in eternity.

The obstacles which make you struggle to spend time with me are making you even stronger because you need me to help. Depend upon me and I will provide. I'm always right there with you. I love you.

Lovingly,

Your heavenly Father, the King

Lesson 6

OUR EXAMPLE
Pray Like Jesus Did

Who better to teach us about prayer than Jesus, the Son of God, himself. Jesus prayed to his Father and he tells us to do the same. Just as Jesus didn't pray using a formula or rules, he doesn't want us to approach the Father fearing we aren't doing it "right." He wants us to pray from the heart.

Yet that's scary because sometimes "rules" and formulas make us feel more secure. If we can do it "right," we might earn some favor or ability to approach God thinking we'll get the answer we want.

But Jesus' example is one of approaching God as one who loves us and knows what's best—not one to be coerced through following "prayer rules." Let's learn from Jesus.

- How do you define a "prayer warrior"?

    ◦ Do you consider yourself one? How does your answer make you feel?

- To what degree do you try to earn something good from God through following some kind of rules or formulas for prayer?

• What does Jesus say about prayer in the following verses?

- Mark 11:22-24:

- John 4:24:

- John 14:13-14:

- John 15:7:

- What difficulty do you have believing these verses?

- What might happen if we take these verses out of context and fail to compare them with all the scriptural teaching on prayer?

When we take a verse or verses out of the context of a passage or the truths expressed throughout the Bible, we can easily believe lies. Based on Jesus' words in other verses, Jesus doesn't want us to just claim anything we want and demand it happen. He also isn't saying we should demand what we're convinced is best.

• What other essential aspects do these verses urge us to consider in knowing how to pray for God's will to be done?

- Psalm 37:4:

- ○ John 14:13:

- ○ John 15:7:

- ○ Have you left any of those out in considering having your prayers answered?

- When Jesus had a decision to make, what did he do (Luke 6:12)?

  - ○ Why do you think Jesus considered prayer more important than meeting the needs of the people (Luke 5:15-16)?

  - ○ What message(s) do those two passages give you?

  - ○ What change(s) do you need to make to be more like Jesus in this area?

We can only imagine the reactions of the people Jesus left behind who were needy. Some may have traveled great distances to be healed or have their emotional needs met. Of course we know Jesus loved every one of them but he also couldn't fulfill what his Father wanted him to do without having time in prayer.

When the needs of others and the pressures of other people's expectations seem to outweigh being strengthened by spending time with God, we can remember Jesus' example.

- Read the following verses and complete the chart.

Passage	Situation	Why/What Jesus Prayed
Mark 6:45-46		
Luke 4:40-44		
Luke 10:17-24		
Luke 22:14-20		
Luke 22:31-32		
Luke 22:39-44		

Passage	Situation	Why/What Jesus Prayed
Luke 23:33-34, 46		
John 11:41-44		
John 12:27-28		

- ○ How will Jesus' prayer or example help you pray during similar situations?

- When Jesus wanted to renew himself, he departed into a desert place often taking the disciples with him. What is significant to you about Mark 6:30-31?

We can easily be tempted to think busyness in the Lord's service represents spiritual devotion. At times, we may even be praised for our "dedication" to God. But Jesus never succumbed to such a false belief. He only did what his Father wanted him to do, not what people valued or thought as spiritual.

Jesus recognized the physical and emotional toll ministry had upon his disciples and provided for their refreshment and strengthening. His expectations were reasonable and sensitive. Of course, it's possible God will invite us into a time of going beyond what seems to be our human capability, but usually it's for a limited time. During that time, we'll learn to a greater degree God's power is sufficient.

- When we pray, we are spending time with Jesus. Read Luke 10:38-42. How does Jesus' reply to Martha speak to you about the time you spend in prayer and read the Bible?

- Read John 17. What two groups of people did Jesus pray for (vss. 9, 20)?

  ○ Who is not included in his prayer (vs. 9)?

  ○ Are you included in the people referred to in verse 20? If not, why not?

Even though we've already talked about this topic in this study, you may not have been ready to commit your life to Christ but now you are. If you would like to ask Jesus into your life as Lord and Savior because you recognize your sin separates you from him (and thus be included in those of verse 20), your prayer of repentance is the only way you can claim Jesus' redemption. Here is a prayer you can consider praying if it is your heart's desire:

Heavenly Father, thank you for loving me so much you sent Jesus to die in my place on the cross. I know I am a sinner, and I do want you to forgive my sins and make me one of your children. I believe Jesus is your Son and conquered death rising from the grave. Come into my life right now to be my Lord and Savior. Thank you for saving me. In Jesus' name. Amen.

- If you believe Jesus is God and he died on the cross for your sins and you asked him to forgive you, what can you be assured of (I John 5:11-13)?

- What did Jesus pray for every believer in John 17?

    o vs. 11:

    o vs. 13:

    o vs. 15:

    o vs. 17:

    o vss. 21-23:

    o vs. 24:

    o vs. 26:

    o Which aspect of his prayer for you is most meaningful? Why?

    o Of those desires Jesus has for you, which do you need the most assurance in believing?

> ○   Is it difficult for you to believe Jesus can fulfill those plans for you? If so, which one(s) and why?

Sometimes we can be surprised at what isn't included in Jesus' prayers—especially this one for those who followed him while he was on earth and future believers who are us (vs. 20). Notice he doesn't pray for what our culture considers valuable: wealth, prosperity, success, achievements, or human glory. Jesus prays for an eternal perspective regarding those things along with spiritual security and a sense of belonging in the kingdom. Plus, he desires we bring glory to God through expressing joy, love, and other spiritual qualities.

Such blessings are priceless. They are not dependent upon people or self-effort, but upon abiding in God's power. Since he wants to grant those things to us, we can be confident of our growth in those areas.

- How is Jesus' prayer in John 17 a model for your prayers for others?

- Who will you pray for this week based on Jesus' prayer?

Any number of verses and passages in the Bible can be prayed for ourselves and other people. We can put someone's name into the verses and pray with courage because we know God wants to answer "yes" to his Son's requests.

- What can we learn about a Christian perspective of life from these verses in John 17:

    ○   vs. 8:

- o vs. 14a:

- o vs. 16:

- o vs. 17b:

- o vs. 18:

- o vs. 19:

- o Which of those perspectives need to be stronger in your life?

- What do the following verses from John 17 say about the relationship between Jesus and his Father, God?

  - o vs. 5:

  - o vs. 10:

  - o vss. 11, 21:

  - o vss. 23-24, 26:

  - o vs. 25:

  - o Are any of those surprising to you? Why?

- From all you've studied in this lesson, why do you think Jesus prayed to his Father?

- Why should we pray to the Father in Jesus' name?

The very fact Jesus prayed in so many different situations and for so many different things—in fact, everything—urges us to know God wants us to pray about everything also.

Our enemy, Satan, wants us to believe our loving Father is only interested in the "big" or "important" challenges of life. After all, isn't God too busy to pay attention to those "little" things concerning us?

Satan also wickedly whispers, "God helps those who help themselves." But Jesus who had all power, even to call thousands of angels to deliver him from the cross, called upon his Father and didn't depend upon his own human efforts.

What an encouragement to know every situation, challenge, person, trial—everything—is of interest to our Father God.

My precious Princess and Daughter,

I HEARD MY SON'S PRAYER FOR YOU. His every word came right from my heart and my desires for you. Everything Jesus is doing right now at my right hand springs from my desires and love for you. He loves you and defends you against your enemy's accusations before my throne. I know it's hard for you to comprehend, but Jesus and I are One with my Spirit. We are wholly unified in purpose and being.

That's why his prayer for you is my plan for you. Yes, Daughter, beloved and special one, I want you to have peace, joy, patience, and unity with your fellow believers. And to know you have the power to fight the evil one.

How? Because you are a citizen of heaven, my world. You may live in the world of earth, but it needn't control you. When trials besiege you, think *This trial only brings me closer to my Father because I seek him more earnestly. I have an all-powerful defender whose help I can have at any moment. Therefore, I have peace and confidence my Father God is working everything together for my good.*

Indeed, I am doing that very thing. Everything's under control because Jesus prayed for you and is praying for you right now.

Lovingly,

Your heavenly Father, the King

Lesson 7

KNOWING GOD
Touching the Heart of Heaven

Prayer is most often thought of as asking God for help and for providing or protecting ourselves or other people. And certainly, those kinds of prayer are welcomed by God. He encourages us to bring our concerns to him.

But prayer is more than requests—supplications and intercession. It also includes praise. Praise focuses on who God is, his qualities. When we know the truth about God, his very nature, we will have more faith in his loving intentions for us and greater trust knowing he knows what's best for us.

Let's focus now on this aspect of prayer: praising God. And we'll focus on it again in a very practical way in our last lesson.

- What percentage of your prayer time focuses on praising God and meditating on his qualities?

  - What do you think is the difference between thanking God and praising him?

Both praise and thanksgiving are valuable aspects of focusing on God. It could be easy to think of them as the same. But praise is focusing on who God is, the attributes of his nature. Giving thanks focuses on what he has done and is doing. In a sense thanksgiving is expressing appreciation for the results of his nature.

Certainly, there's nothing bad or wrong about "mixing" them, but if we distinguish between them, our prayer time and relationship with God can be even more dynamic and varied.

- Read Luke 1:46-55. Mary praised God and she gave thanks for what he had accomplished. From each verse, indicate which she did (or both) and what she described.

Luke 1:46-55	Mary's Thanksgiving	Mary's Praise
vs. 46		
vs. 47		
vs. 48		

Luke 1:46-55	Mary's Thanksgiving	Mary's Praise
vs. 49		
vs. 50		
vs. 51		
vs. 52		
vs. 53		
vs. 54		

Luke 1:46-55	Mary's Thanksgiving	Mary's Praise
vs. 55		

- Of the truths Mary recognized about God, which one do you appreciate the most? Express it here by finishing the sentence,

  - Heavenly Father, I praise you because you are:

  - Heavenly Father, I thank you because you have:

- Read Exodus 33:12-13. What was Moses' request?

- "Know" means to grow more deeply and intimately acquainted. How do you think growing in *knowing* God "deeply and intimately" will affect:

  - your prayer life?

  - your faith in God?

  - your relationships with other people?

  - your outreach to unbelievers?

- your contentment?

- coping with stress or worry?

If we don't know God "deeply and intimately," we are believing lies about him. It's easy, especially as children, to begin believing lies about him when difficult or hurtful things occur. We don't know how to combat Satan's false messages of God being untrustworthy, undependable, unloving, or any number of misleading ideas. As adults, we must counteract those lies by focusing on the truth of Scripture that tells us God's qualities.

- After Moses makes his request, how does God answer him in Exodus 33:17?

  - What reasons does God give for saying "yes" to Moses?

  - How do you think God would respond to you if you requested the same thing? Do you want to? Explain.

- Read Psalm 103:7. What do you think is the difference between the *ways* shown to Moses and the *deeds* shown to the Israelites?

- What do the following verses from Exodus say about possible obstacles to the Israelites knowing God's "ways." Also, what were Moses' attitudes enabling him to see God's ways?

Israelites' Attitudes	Moses' Attitudes
14:11-12:	14:13-14:
16:2-3:	16:6-8:
17:2-3:	17:4-6:
20:18-19:	20:20-21:

- o Which obstacles of the Israelites do you find in your life most often?

- o How does Moses' attitudes inspire you to change your thinking?

- What did Paul want other believers to know in Ephesians 1:15-23?

- º vs. 17:

- º vs. 18:

- º vs. 19:

- º vss. 20-21:

- º vss. 22-23:

- º Which of those do you believe the most? Why?

- º Which of those are you weak in believing? Why?

We can be encouraged knowing Paul taught the Ephesian believers in person, yet they still needed to be taught and reminded of the great truths of the Gospel.

- • Read Philippians 3:7-16. What did Paul value most (vs. 8)?

  - º In comparison to that, what was everything else in his life (vs. 8)?

  - º Is there anything more important to you than knowing God? Explain.

  - º What else was important to Paul (vs. 10)? Why would these be significant?

  - º Are they significant in your life?

○ According to verse 12, Paul had not reached those goals perfectly. What does that communicate to you?

○ How did Paul intend to grow closer to his goal of knowing Christ better (vs. 13)?

○ Sometimes we are unsure of whether we are pressing on (vs. 14) in the right direction. What comfort or assurance do verses 15-16 give you?

Even the great apostle Paul is in a process of growth, and in fact, earlier in his letter to the Philippians he writes *And I am sure of this, that he who began a good work in you will bring it to completion at the day of Jesus Christ* (1:6). He doesn't write, "will bring it to completion tomorrow" or "has already done it so be perfect." On this earth, we'll always be learning more about who God is and how to praise him, along with growing in holiness.

• Complete the following chart:

Verse(s)	Attribute(s) of God	How this attribute(s) draws you closer to God
Deuteronomy 32:4		
I Chronicles 29:11-12		
Psalm 34:8		
Psalm 86:5		
Psalm 86:15		
Psalm 147:5		

Verse(s)	Attribute(s) of God	How this attribute(s) draws you closer to God
Isaiah 25:1		
Zephaniah 3:17		
Matthew 11:29		
I John 4:8		

- What shouldn't we boast about and what can we correctly boast about (Jeremiah 9:23-24)?

It may seem logical to boast of things of this world and what mankind values, but all of it is temporary and eventually worthless. Only knowing God in truth and praising him will resound into eternity.

It's hard to distinguish between boasting about ourselves and boasting of God's work in our lives. But pointing out to others how God helped, empowered, or made a difference in our lives is boasting with an eternal perspective.

- Write down qualities or attributes of God on a separate piece of paper, affixing the list in a prominent place in your home. Then you'll be reminded of how you can praise God.

  o Which quality in that list is easiest for you to believe or trust and which is hardest?

  o Which quality or qualities do you seem to believe with your mind but not with your heart?

- Take one of those "difficult to feel" qualities and, using a concordance or Bible software, look up two or three verses about that quality. Write them out and meditate on them for the next week. You may even want to memorize one of those verses and/or write out the verses(s) on cards to be placed in areas of your home.

  o How do you think meditating on that quality will deepen your knowledge of God?

  o Write a prayer of praise to God for that quality.

Learning about who God is and knowing how to praise him is both a gift from God and something we practice. It doesn't necessarily come easily. If it's never been modeled for us on a daily basis, we may not even think of praising God as our day goes along.

Have no fear. God wants you to learn to include thoughts of his qualities because he deserves praise. Also, because he knows it's good for his created ones—you.

Take heart and trust he'll do far more than you can imagine.

My precious Princess and Daughter,

I WANT YOU TO KNOW ME INTIMATELY AND DEEPLY. I want you to know the truth about my nature. As you do—and I know it's a process of always learning more—your trust and faith in me will grow tremendously. You see, my valued Daughter, I am good, loving, kind, merciful, gracious, and a thousand other wonderful qualities. Each one tells you more about me.

You are important and precious to me. Please believe that. I can be trusted. None of my qualities is bad. I intend to draw you closer to me and I cherish every evidence you are becoming more like me every day.

As you get to know me better, you will understand more clearly my workings on this earth. Most people know of what I do. Unfortunately, they often misinterpret my deeds. I want you to know the truth about my ways, which represent my pure, loving heart. And to know my attributes which motivate my ways. Moses longed to know me intimately and he trusted my love. The Israelites were afraid of me. They didn't trust my love. Which will you be like?

Come. Listen to my heart. Celebrate your worship of me because it is grounded in who I am. I want only what's best for you. And your praise honors me while it purifies your heart, driving out sin and doubt, leaving it wide open for me to work and assure you of my love.

Lovingly,

Your heavenly Father, the King

Lesson 8

INTERCESSION
Prayer for Others

Most people think of prayer as praying for the needs of ourselves and others. And it surely is. Although we're learning there are many kinds of prayer and different aspects of it, in this lesson we will concentrate on intercession—praying for others.

Our loving heavenly Father is eager to hear our concerns for ourselves and others. He cares and loves everyone. Even though he knows everything about them because he is omniscient—knowing everything—he still invites us to participate in his work in their lives—and ours. It's one of the mysteries of the spiritual life and the kingdom of God.

Let's see if we can add some insight and understanding into this remarkable privilege of intercession.

- When did you pray for someone else and see a definite
  answer? Explain.

  - What is the most significant "yes" answer to a
    prayer request you have seen?

- ○ What is the most significant "no" answer to a prayer request you have seen?

- Read Matthew 20:20-28. What request did the mother of the sons of Zebedee make to Jesus (vs. 21)?

  - ○ What is your reaction to her?

  - ○ What do you think motivated her?

  - ○ Even though misdirected, what does her request show about her faith?

  - ○ What was a result of her request (vs. 24)?

- What motives do you think are right when we pray for others?

  - ○ Have you ever interceded for the needs of others with a similar motive as this mother?

It might be easy to criticize this mother, but on the good side she did acknowledge and believe Jesus had the power to fulfill her request. She possessed spiritual insights many other people didn't have at that time. Most people saw Jesus' role as Messiah as one which would free the Jews from the rule of the Romans. They weren't concerned about any heavenly kingdom, like she was, only the Jewish kingdom on earth being restored.

We may wonder where this whole idea of the thrones came from. Possibly early in the day, Jesus had talked about that very thing. Matthew 19:28 tells us, *Jesus said to them, "Truly, I say to you, in the new world, when the Son of Man will sit on his glorious throne, you who have followed me will also sit on twelve thrones, judging the twelve tribes of Israel."* So, it wasn't as if the idea wasn't a possibility. It was the placement of the disciples near Jesus the sons of Zebedee and their mother were concerned about.

Some commentators believe her sons prompted her to ask on their behalf. In fact, Mark 10:35-41 describes the sons asking. Most likely all three of them spoke up. After all, most of us could reason in a situation like that, there's more persuasion in many voices.

We don't know if this loving mother desired to ask or if she felt pressured by her sons. Most mothers might be eager to make such a request because they want the best for their children—even if it's in eternity. How commendable she had spiritual vision to think of eternity and God's throne; curiously, she didn't ask for anything for herself. We might have desired to at least ask for a footstool to sit on at Jesus' feet.

- What prayer command does James 5:16 give us?

  ○ What results from effective prayer (James 5:16-17)?

  ○ Why do you think God gave us this example of Elijah here? Read I Kings 17:1.

Although God most likely won't request we pray regarding whether it rains (or maybe he will), James wants to emphasize the earnestness of Elijah and his example of faith.

- What did Paul pray for fellow believers?

  ○ Romans 15:5-6:

- o I Thessalonians 5:23:

- o II Thessalonians 1:11-12:

- o II Thessalonians 2:16-17:

- o Hebrews 13:20-21:

- o Which of those truths/insights/prayers is needed by you?

- o By a friend of yours?

- o Write a prayer for your friend or yourself.

- Read Ephesians 1:15-19. What did Paul want the Ephesians:

  - o to know:

  - o to grow in understanding about:

- Again from Ephesians 1:15-19, what do you think these phrases mean?

  - o "eyes of your heart may be enlightened":

  - o "hope to which he has called you":

  - o "riches of his glorious inheritance in the saints":

- o "great power for us who believe":

- Read Ephesians 3:14-19. How would prayer strengthen you with power in your inner being (vs. 16)?

  - o The word "dwell" means "be at home in" (vs. 17). How would Christ's presence in your life ground your prayer life in love?

  - o How would the love of Christ enable you to be filled with the fulness of God? How does prayer affect that (vs. 18-19)?

- Read Philippians 1:9-11. What did Paul pray for the Philippian believers?

  - o What do his requests mean to you?

  - o How can you follow his example in your prayers?

  - o Read Galatians 5:22-23. Why do you think Paul mentioned the fruits of righteousness in Philippians 1:11 as part of his prayer for the Philippians?

  - o What is the fruit of righteousness that gives glory and praise to God (vs. 11)?

  - o Who do you know who needs these verses prayed for them?

- Read Colossians 1:9-12. How does Paul's consistent praying inspire you (vs. 9)?

  ○ What did Paul want the Colossians to be filled with (vs. 9)?

  ○ When we have wisdom and understanding, what five things will happen (vs. 10-11a)?

  ○ When those things happen, what three things result (vs. 11c-12)?

  ○ What is one reason we should thank God (vs. 12)?

  ○ Who will you pray this passage for?

  ○ What do the elements of Paul's prayer teach you about how and what you should pray for?

Obviously, because of all the specific things Paul says he prays for others, we can never say we don't know what to pray for others or ourselves. Paul wants to encourage his readers when they know what he is praying for them and for them to know how to pray for others. But God knew these examples would empower Christians through the centuries to pray powerfully.

We might be tempted to think we shouldn't use such a "crutch" in our prayers as the prayers of others. It might even seem inauthentic or ingenuous to use someone else's wording. But God loves to hear his Word being brought before him. He looks at our hearts and our motives. If we are praying God's Word with a desire to see God work in the lives of ourselves and others, he hears and responds.

A part of prayer is thanking God for what he has done in others' lives. Fill out this chart with Paul's reasons for thanksgiving and a person for whom you could give thanks in that same category.

Verse(s)	Thanks for	Person
Romans 1:8		
Ephesians 1:15-16		
Philippians 1:2-6		
Colossians 1:3-4		
II Thessalonians 1:3-4		

Verse(s)	Thanks for	Person
II Timothy 1:3-5		

- Who should we pray for in addition to friends and family (I Timothy 2:1-2)?

  o What should we pray for them?

  o What should we do to have God answer our prayers about our nation (II Chronicles 7:14)?

- What should we pray for those in ministry?

  o Ephesians 6:18-20:

  o Colossians 4:3-4:

  o II Thessalonians 3:1-2:

  o Write a prayer for a person you know who ministers to others.

- What can we pray for unbelievers (Acts 26:18)?

- In your own words, pray those things for someone you know who doesn't know Christ as Savior. Write out your prayer.

• How can you be more faithful in praying for others?

Our loving God must have known we would feel intimidated about praying for ourselves and others. The Word of God provides more than enough ideas of what God wants to hear in our prayers and wishes to provide through our prayers.

You may have noticed most of those ideas are for a person's spiritual walk. Of course, he wants to provide basic needs but primarily, he is interested in our relationship with him. From such a rich connection, every good thing blossoms.

My precious Princess and Daughter,

HOW I DELIGHT IN HEARING YOU PRAY FOR OTHERS—AND YOURSELF. Your motives may not always be perfectly selfless, but your supplications for others please me. You may not realize it, but when you come to me focused on the needs of others, you are increasing your own faith and dependence upon me. As a result, you also will be changed to be more in the image of my Son, Jesus—just like those you're praying for.

What joy it gives me to answer these prayers. Pray for their spiritual, emotional and mental growth often. Surround my throne with your prayers.

But keep in mind I will not force anyone to do anything. I'm sure that's frustrating to you at times. But please remember, precious Daughter, I am the only One who can meet all your needs. If you are praying for them to change so that your life can be less troublesome, certainly you can see the wrong motives in that. Instead, yearn for their spiritual growth—not because you will be less inconvenienced but because they will fall more in love with me.

In the meantime, I promise to meet your needs, too. Remember my plans for you are for your good and never for your harm. Keep your eyes focused on me.

Lovingly,

Your heavenly Father, the King

Lesson 9

GRATITUDE
Humility in Thanksgiving

At times, we can be so full of gratitude to God and other times we feel down-in-the-dumps like there's nothing we can give thanks for. It's difficult to not let our feelings pull down what we know is true: God is good all the time and deserves our gratitude.

We would expect the Word of God to talk a lot about gratitude and indeed it does. We will be inspired from this lesson on focusing on the many blessings we can enjoy from God—even if something isn't exactly the way we'd prefer. That's why we need to remember gratitude is not based on our circumstances but upon the faithful love of our heavenly Father.

- What are you most thankful about as you think of God's work in your life?

- How did Jesus show his gratitude in Matthew 14:19, 26:26?

- Read Judges 4-5. What causes Deborah and Barak to sing praise and thanksgiving to God?

  - Is this a prayer? Why or why not? What specific things do they say?

Although there are not harmonious opinions among theologians and commentators, some believe Deborah and Barak sang different portions back and forth. Some also think a chorus of men participated in the singing. But in almost one accord, they believe Deborah was the primary composer of the work.

- As you complete the following chart, ask yourself if you've experienced a stressful situation or temptation where God provided victory, deliverance or help.

Judges 5 Verses	Summary	Applied to my life
2-5	Praise for past help	
6-8	Current stressful situation	
9-18	Who God used to help	
19-27	How he helped	

Judges 5 Verses	Summary	Applied to my life
28-31	Victory is celebrated	
32	Future victories	

The Word of God is relevant for everyday living and everything we experience. His words always point to who God is and his work in our lives giving us plenty of reasons to be grateful. But gratitude is a choice. So often after God works, we take his involvement for granted and might even take credit ourselves.

Deborah resisted thinking she had created the army's success. She accepted God's empowering and didn't forget he was the source, not her own ingenuity, experience, wisdom, or intelligence. God was the total source because then he was glorified, which was Deborah's motive for singing her song and being grateful.

- What do you think a "sacrifice of praise" means (Hebrews 13:15)?

  - How does Psalm 51:14-17 help to explain that phrase?

  - Why is praise linked to thanksgiving?

God instituted the sacrificial system as recorded in the Old Testament. The Israelites kept those laws as the way to serve and honor God. Although God wanted his people's hearts to be "into" the giving of their sacrifices, most of the time they kept the laws as a means of earning his favor. They then felt entitled to receive God's blessings. Their sacrifices lacked gratitude for God's gracious love—since they believed they had earned his gifts.

The sacrifices were meant to point to the future when the Messiah would arrive and sacrifice himself to take away sins. God wanted their hearts to be grateful and praising him because he would provide everything for their redemption.

When Jesus rose from the grave indicating God's plan had been completed, the Old Testament-kind-of sacrifices were no longer needed. Instead God made it possible for his believers to offer sacrifices of the heart: through praise and thanksgiving for all he had done on their behalf. Such gratitude motivated the surrender of their own lives in service to him.

Thanksgiving, the deepest kind, is fueled by recognizing we are helpless in ourselves to save ourselves or have the power we need to live righteous and selfless lives. It is God's total gift of grace making it possible. Knowing such truth puts the emphasis where it should be: we're no longer grateful for our own efforts but for his power in us.

- What did the following women have reason to thank God for?

Passage	Who	Why
Mark 5:25-34		
Mark 7:24-30		
Mark 12:41-44		
Luke 2:36-38		
Luke 2:39-52		

Passage	Who	Why
Luke 7:36-50		
John 4:1-30		
John 8:1-11		

- o Which of these situations is most meaningful to you? Why?

- • What do the following verses say we should thank God for?

  - o Romans 1:8:

  - o I Corinthians 15:57:

  - o II Corinthians 2:14:

  - o II Corinthians 9:11-12:

- ◦ II Thessalonians 1:3:

- ◦ I Timothy 1:12-17:

- ◦ Are you currently thanking God for any of those? Explain.

Giving thanks or "being" thankful is often thought of as something we must feel, but we may not always "feel" grateful. We can still express our thanks to God. In its simplest form, thanksgiving is choosing to acknowledge God as the source of what happened and is in charge of everything happening to us. Of course, such a choice can be very difficult considering he allows challenging things. But after Adam and Eve sinned, God's original plan to have earth be our "forever" place of joy in his presence ended because perfect relationship with God had been destroyed by sin. The fulfillment God had originally designed which they found in the Garden would never be experienced again on earth. Humanity could only look forward to the perfection and fulfillment of being in God's presence in heaven.

If we are counting on the meager things of earth to be worthy of gratitude, we won't find much. Of course, God does generously provide a taste of joy on this earth. But counting on future total joy gives us a perspective supporting choosing gratitude for whatever God provides on earth each day.

- • What are we to thank God for according to these verses?

Verse(s)	Thing	Reason/Result
Romans 5:2-5		
II Corinthians 7:8-10		
I Peter 1:6-7		
I Peter 4:12-14		
James 1:2-4		
James 1:9		

Verse(s)	Thing	Reason/Result
James 1:12		

- ○ Which of those is most difficult for you to rejoice in?

- ○ How could you make a change in your perspective?

- Read Philippians 4:6-7. Why do you think thanksgiving is an essential part of not being anxious?

  - ○ How do thanksgiving and Philippians 4:8 connect?

  - ○ How does Philippians 4:8 help support the concepts of Philippians 4:6-7?

Worry is often the result of fearful and negative thinking. Worry feeds on an absence of gratitude and acknowledging God is good, regardless if what we fear might happen. Gratitude in effect says *Thank you, Lord, you know what you're doing. I can choose to release fear and trust knowing you intend this for my good and your glory.*

Although we might not initially think of it this way, being grateful to God is a form of prayer. Any time we are directing our attention to God, we are praying. And gratitude invites God into our lives by acknowledging his sovereignty, even in difficult circumstances.

- Read Philippians 4:11-13. How is contentment related to choosing gratitude for God's will?

  ○ Although Paul doesn't use any words related to thanksgiving, how is he being grateful?

  ○ What is the basis for his perspective?

- What is your response to the fact even the Apostle Paul had to "learn" to be content, a form of gratitude?

  ○ How does Philippians 4:19 support Paul's form of gratitude in verses 11-13?

Paul didn't base his attitude on everything always going well or according to his preferences. He *learned* to be content. It's often easy to condemn ourselves for our lack of gratitude and acknowledgment of God. Our faith can seem weak when we can't regard God as always good because life doesn't seem to be "good." Paul shows us gratitude and contentment aren't based on feelings, but a choice and something we grow in.

If there is something in your life you find difficult to thank God for, write a prayer to God expressing your feelings. If possible, make a choice each day this week to thank God even though you don't "feel" like it. And praise him, too.

My precious Princess and Daughter,

YOUR PRAISE AND GRATITUDE ARE DELIGHTFUL GIFTS YOU GIVE ME. I know the difficult situations and people in your life. When you refuse to give in to bitterness, anger, and doubt and instead choose to trust me enough to praise and thank me, I am delighted. That's my Daughter!

Not only do I want you to praise me for who I am, I want you to thank me for what I do. Both of these disciplines deepen our relationship. And you experience a greater appreciation of who I am.

When you acknowledge the truth about me, you will believe nothing is beyond my capabilities or power. At times, I choose to limit my workings, but I am incapable of wrong things like sinning and tempting you.

So, let your life thank me. Rejoice in my position in your life, my love for you, and my power. Tell me your gratitude through music, words, and poetry, boasting to others of who I am and what I do in your life. You may "brag" to others about your loving Father. Feel good praising me; don't feel guilty. I created you to fulfill such a high calling—acknowledging my good work in your life. No wonder you enjoy thanking me. It's what you were made for.

Lovingly,

Your heavenly Father, the King

Lesson 10

PRAISE
Our God's Right

As we've learned, praise is acknowledging who God is. We've addressed many aspects of how praise connects us with God. Knowing and speaking of his attributes out loud or in prayer glorifies him and fights against the lies Satan whispers. We know our loving heavenly Father is pleased, not because he is some sinfully proud ogre demanding groveling but because he knows we truly are meant to praise him and it's good for us.

Yes, it's true, praise is his right because he is supremely and completely holy, good, and rightly motivated. But he also designed our hearts to be encouraged and uplifted by concentrating on his glories. Let's do that more in this last lesson by learning more how to express our praise.

- When you praise God, how do you feel?

  ○ Have you ever felt like your praise was inadequate? Why?

- Read Acts 2:42-47. What evidence of unselfishness accompanied the praise of God in the early Christian believers?

- Study the Scriptures below. What about God are we to praise?

    o I Chronicles 29:11-13:

    o Psalm 21:13:

    o Psalm 89:5:

    o Psalm 138:2-8:

    o Psalm 145:4-5:

    o What qualities, actions, or attributes of God would you add to this list?

- Read Psalm 46.

    o Verses 1-3 talk about God's power. Write out what his power means to you and praise him for it.

    o Verses 4-7 talk about God's presence. Write out what his presence means to you and praise him for it.

    o Verses 8-11 talk about God's peace. Write out what his peace means to you and praise him for it.

You have just written your own psalm. Congratulations. Isn't it wonderful how God inspires us through his love letter to us? His love letter is the Bible and it teaches us in so many ways. Our gracious

Almighty God made sure we have plenty to praise him about and even gave us examples to learn from. He thinks of everything.

- Psalm 23 is probably the most famous and beloved of all psalms. Re-write each verse in your own words using a current problem or challenge you are facing. Remember, God delights in whatever your own God-given-creativity produces.

    o vs. 1:

    o vs. 2:

    o vs. 3:

    o vs. 4:

    o vs. 5:

    o vs. 6:

The singers and composers of the Psalms are in effect, praising God whether they use the word "praise" or not. Even in the psalms which express unpleasant feelings like depression (Psalms 42, 43), they are still giving praise because they are acknowledging trust in who God is—and as someone who can be trusted.

- Write your own psalm using these prompts as a guide:

Lord God, you are…

I bless your holy name because…

Even though there is much trouble or pain around me, I…

I have seen your power and help in former times when…

I want to always…

Thank you, Lord God Almighty for…

I know you are…

And worthy to be praised.

- Read Luke 1:46-55. Using Mary's Song as a pattern, write your own Song of Praise to God, and magnify, worship, and praise him.

  ○ Tell him what you appreciate about his attributes (vss. 46-47):

  ○ Tell him what you appreciate about his care of you or his actions on your behalf (vss. 48-49):

  ○ Tell him what promise from Scripture you want to claim or have already claimed (vs. 50):

  ○ Review how you have seen him work in the lives of unbelievers (vs. 51):

  ○ Review how you've seen him work in your community, state, or country (vs. 52):

o   Review how you've seen him help those who trust
    in him (vss. 53-55):

o   Close with your personal, direct words of praise
    and thanksgiving to him.

Have some of these exercises encouraged you? It's possible they have discouraged you. Everyone will have different responses. Writing out or thinking along these lines can be very challenging. For some it comes easily, especially if a woman enjoys writing down her thoughts.

If you are not one of them, don't allow Satan to bring condemnation or self-contempt into your mind and heart. God loves to receive from you whatever you can offer, even if it's one sentence; even if you write or say, *Lord, I don't know how to praise you but I want to learn.* He knows your heart anyway and he delights to teach and lead you through the power of his Spirit within you. Be assured of his patience. He doesn't have unrealistic expectations. He knows the cry of your heart.

•   In heaven, all praise God. From the book of Revelations,
    who does that and what do they say?

Verse(s)	Who	What
4:8		

Verse(s)	Who	What
4:10-11		
5:8-10		
5:11-12		
5:13		
5:14		
7:9-10		

Verse(s)	Who	What
7:11-12		
11:16-17		
15:1-4		
16:4-7		
19:1-3, 6-7		

- ° After reading such great exaltation of God, how would you praise God? Write it out.

- How will you continue to use praise as a part of your prayerful fellowship with God?

My precious Princess and Daughter,

I UNDERSTAND WHEN YOU FEEL YOUR WORDS ARE INADEQUATE TO PRAISE ME. But, my beloved Daughter, I look at your heart. I see what can't be expressed in words. Whether you are making requests, crying out in pain, confessing your sins, praising me, or thanking me, I love it all because it is my daughter's gift to me. I take delight in your efforts to reach out to me, to please me, to honor me. So, don't belittle your efforts, I don't.

Precious Daughter, even when you feel far away from me, please remember I am always here for you. You are never too far away spiritually to be reunited with me. My mercy and grace are unlimited. I am the God of a thousand second chances. You are mine.

Yes, I am mighty and terrible. I am a God of righteous judgment as well as mercy. Rejoice in all my attributes. Each one gives you a reason to trust me and a reason to praise me. Each one works in your life for your good. Every time you tell someone else how to become part of our family, you praise me. Tell others how I can be their Savior and Lord. I hear every cry for forgiveness and salvation—the best kind of prayer.

Let the words of your mouth and the thoughts of your heart honor me. I love you. I love hearing from you, whether or not you think your words are adequate. I applaud every word and encourage you to continue. I am worthy of all praise, no matter how expressed.

Lovingly,

Your heavenly Father, the King

www.ingramcontent.com/pod-product-compliance
Lightning Source LLC
Chambersburg PA
CBHW060312050426
42448CB00009B/1802